MORALITY, GOODNESS, GOOD KARMA, SPIRITUALITY AND SOUL

THIRD EDITION

An interpretation of the Bhagavad Gita.
ISBN: 9781399915090

BY PROF. NARESH SETHI

info@altruisticmind.com or nsethi4@yahoo.com
www.altruisticmind.com

TABLE OF CONTENTS

INTRODUCTION

---※---

The 'Bhagavad-gita', one of the main founding books of Vedic knowledge/ Hinduism (it was written after the other 2 main scriptures of Sanatana Dharma, The Vedas and The Upanishads).

It was about 5 thousand years ago that Lord Krishna spoke 'Bhagavad-gita' to His friend Arjuna. It was just after this time of the Mahabharata when the present age of Kali began (Kali = Kalyug- age of quarrel and strife with less virtue and goodness).

Their discourse is regarded as one of the greatest philosophical and religious dialogues known to man; it took place just before the onset of war between the Kauravas (the hundreds of sons of Dhrtarastra) and the Pandavas (the sons of Pandu). Dhrtarastra and Pandu were brothers; it was a war between cousins. The Pandavas had returned from 13 years of exile and rightfully demanded their kingdom back from the Kauravas. The Kauravas refused and granted not even 5 villages to the 5 Pandava brothers - there was no choice but to go to war. The Kauravas snatched Krishna's armies but the Pandavas had Krishna as advisor, helper, guide and charioteer of Arjuna's chariot - Lord Krishna sided with the Pandavas who were men of high morals.

The Pandavas who put their trust in the hands of Lord Krishna won the battle.

KARMA YOGA

Karma Yoga is the performance of one's duties without expectation of reward. Working to live, without attachment to lust, passion or undue rewards is important, fulfilling and exemplary to others.

One should perform one's duties without expectation of material reward. Working to live for bare necessities, one is not affected by sinful reactions.

Without being attached to the fruits of activities one should act as a matter of duty, for by working without attachment one attains the Supreme.

It is everyone's duty to work and not need to depend on any other living being. This also sets an example to others to work and be independent.

If I (Krishna) did not perform prescribed duties, all these worlds would be put to ruination. I would be the cause of creating unwanted population, and I would thereby destroy the peace of all living beings.

The learned should guide the ignorant who work just for fruits, into religion & spiritual activity and not be bound by the reactions of work,

Lust and passion and transform into wrath, which is the all-devouring sinful enemy of the world. Lust covers the real knowledge of the living entity and bewilders them.

Therefore, O Arjuna, best of the Bharatas, in the very beginning curb this great symbol of sin [lust] by regulating the senses, and slay this destroyer of knowledge & self-realization.

The working senses are superior to dull matter; mind is higher than the senses; intelligence is still higher than the mind; and he [the soul] is even higher than the intelligence. One should steady the mind by deliberate spiritual intelligence [Krishna consciousness] and thus-by spiritual strength - conquer this insatiable enemy known as lust.

TRANSCENDENTAL KNOWLEDGE

This refers to the <u>spiritual existence</u> of matter and the being - neither born nor ever deteriorated. God (Krishna) appears frequently, millennium after millennium when there is irreligion or lack of order. Krishna is the unborn and his transcendental body never deteriorates, and although he is the Lord of all entities, he still appears in every millennium in His original transcendental form.

"Whenever and wherever there is a decline in religious practice, (O descendant of Bharata,) and a predominant rise of irreligion - at that time I descend Myself.

To deliver the pious and to annihilate the miscreants, as well as to re-establish the principles of religion, I Myself appear millennium after millennium."

One who <u>knows</u> the transcendental nature of My appearance and activities does not, upon leaving the body, take his birth again in this material world, but attains My eternal abode.

One should be free from attachment, fear and anger, be fully absorbed in Krishna & take refuge in Krishna, thus becoming purified & attaining transcendental love for God. Surrender unto Krishna.

Some desiring success in fruitive activities worship the demigods, even offering sacrifices; quickly they may get results & it is good to be friends with demigods but to attain Krishna is better.

Being fully absorbed in Krishna ensures one attains the spiritual nature and kingdom.

Some people who try to achieve self-realization through control of the mind & senses, offer the functions of all the senses, and of the life breath, as oblations into the fire of the controlled mind. Some offer their possessions and perform yoga of eightfold mysticism, or by studying the Vedas to advance in transcendental knowledge. Some do breathing Yoga exercises; some curtail eating (much) using their breathing exercises.

All these can become cleansed of sinful reactions, and, having tasted the nectar of the results of sacrifices, they can advance toward the supreme eternal atmosphere.

Without sacrifice one cannot live happily on this planet, what then of the next?

Just try to learn the Truth by approaching a spiritual master, inquire from him submissively and render service to him. The self-realized souls can impart knowledge into you because they have seen the truth.

Having obtained real knowledge from a self-realized soul, you will never fall again into such illusion, for by this knowledge you will see that all living beings are but part of the Supreme, or, in other words, that they are Mine. Those who renounce fruits of actions, act in devotional service through transcendental knowledge and can help sinners cross over the ocean of miseries to Me.

Thus, he is not bound by the reactions of work, 0 conqueror of the riches. Doubts arisen in your heart out of ignorance should be slashed by the weapon of knowledge. [Armed with Yoga, 0 Bharata, stand & fight].

KARMA YOGA & KRSNA CONSCIOUSNESS

Work in the performance of one prescribed duties - without expectation of undue reward or passion, lust, etc; - plus devotional service to Krishna is best.

Devotional service to Krishna & work in devotion is better than work to survive or work for material gains, fruits & passions. Working in devotion one surrenders the results to God.

When one's intelligence, mind, faith and refuge are all fixed in the Supreme, then one becomes fully cleansed of misgivings through complete knowledge and thus one proceeds straight to the path of liberation. Such a liberated person is not attracted to material sense pleasure but is always in trance, enjoying the pleasure within. In this way the self-realized person enjoys unlimited happiness, for he concentrates on the Supreme.

Those who are free from anger and material desires, who are self-realized, self-disciplined and constantly endeavouring for perfection, are assured of liberation in the Supreme in the very near future.

One has to shut out all external sense objects, keeping the eyes and vision concentrated between the two eyebrows, suspending the inward and outward breaths within the nostrils, and thus controlling the mind, senses and intelligence, the transcendental being, aiming at liberation becomes free from desire, fear and anger. One who is always in this state is certainly liberated. Concentrating on Me the Supreme Lord of all planets & demigods, the benefactor & well-wisher of all living entities, one attains peace from the pangs of material miseries.

DHYANA-YOGA

Yoga and Meditation with focus on the supreme are important in achieving (devotional connection) oneness with God. Meditate in a quiet place, unagitated mind devoid of fear, lust & passion.

A person is said to be elevated in Yoga when, having renounced all material desires, he neither acts for sense gratification nor engages in fruitive activities. For him who has conquered the mind, the mind is the best of friends; but for one who has failed to do so, his very mind will remain the greatest enemy. For one who has conquered the mind, the Supersoul is already reached, for he has attained tranquillity. To such a man happiness and distress, heat & cold, honour and dishonour are all the same. One should practice yoga in a quiet secluded place, control his mind, senses & activities and fix the mind on one point. With an unagitated, subdued mind, devoid of fear, free from sex life, one should meditate on Me within the heart & make Me the ultimate goal of life. If the mind wanders, bring it back as it is very difficult to curb the restless mind.

Successful Yogis reach and unite with Krishna; unsuccessful yogis are reborn in aristocratic or even better pious families.

KNOWLEDGE OF THE ABSOLUTE

Of the 4 kinds of devotional service "Searching for the knowledge of the Absolute" is the best; others are out of distress, being inquisitive or for seeking wealth. Devotional service to the Lord may release you from old age or death.

There is no truth superior to Krishna. Everything rests upon Krishna, as pearls are strung on a thread. Earth, water, fire, air, ether, mind, intelligence & false ego together constitute His separated material energies.

He is the origin & dissolution of all material things.

He is the taste of water, the light of the sun and the moon, the syllable Oṁ in the Vedic mantras; He is the sound in ether and ability in man.

Four kinds of pious men begin to render devotional service unto Me - the distressed, the desirous of wealth, the inquisitive, and he who is searching for knowledge of the Absolute. Of these, the one who is always engaged in pure devotional service is the best; attaining transcendental service he is sure to attain me. Those who benefit from worshipping demigods benefit from me (via them). The fruits are limited & temporary & they go to the planets of the demigods, but My devotees ultimately reach My supreme planet.

I am never manifest to the foolish and unintelligent.

"O Arjuna, as the Supreme Personality of Godhead, I know everything that has happened in the past, all that is happening in the present, and all things that are yet to come. I also know all living entities; but Me no one knows. Pious people engage in My service with determination. Intelligent persons who are endeavouring for liberation from old age and death take refuge in Me in devotional service.

ATTAINING THE SUPREME

One who mediates on the Supreme Personality of Godhead, consistently, constantly and un-deviated from the path, reaches the Supreme (Lord)

Whoever, at the end of his life, quits his body, remembering Me alone, at once attains My nature. The Yogic situation is that of detachment from all sensual engagements. Closing all the doors of the senses and fixing the mind on the heart and the life air at the top of the head, one establishes himself in Yoga. In such a state thinking of Me he will reach the spiritual planets, (so fight Arjuna, thinking of Me)

From the highest planet in the material world down to the lowest, all are places of misery wherein repeated birth and death take place. But one who attains to My abode, 0 son of Kunti, never takes birth again.

By human calculation, a thousand ages taken together form the duration of Brahma's one day. And such also is the duration of his night.

When Brahma's day arrives, all living entities come into being, and with the arrival of Brahma's night they are helplessly annihilated.

A person who accepts the path of devotional service is not bereft of the results derived from studying the Vedas, performing austere sacrifices, giving charity or pursuing philosophical and fruitive activities. By performing devotional service, he attains these & reaches the supreme eternal abode.

THE MOST CONFIDENTIAL KNOWLEDGE

I am the father of this universe, the mother, the support, and the grandsire. I am the object of knowledge, the purifier and the syllable Om; I am also the Rg, the Sama of the Yajur Vedas. I am the very source of creation rather than part of its cosmic manifestation. Worshiping me is Supreme and one who does so attains me; those who worship demigods actually worship only me but they may take birth among the demigods; others seeking enjoyment and Vedic principles only achieve repeated birth and death.

By Me, in My unmanifested form, this entire universe is pervaded. All beings are in Me.

And yet everything that is created does not rest in Me. Behold My mystic opulence! Although I am the maintainer of all living entities, and although I am everywhere, I am not a part of this cosmic manifestation, for My Self is the very source of creation.

As the mighty wind, blowing everywhere, rests always in the sky, all created beings rest in Me.

The great souls that perpetually & devotionally worship Me, attain me. Others cultivate the knowledge to worship Me.

I am the father of this universe, the mother, the support, and the grandsire. I am the object of knowledge, the purifier and the syllable Oṁ. I am also the Ṛg, the Sâma, and the Yajur Vedas.

It is I who am the ritual, I the sacrifice, the offering to the ancestors, the healing herb, the transcendental chant. I am the butter and the fire and the offering.

I am the goal, the sustainer, the master, the witness, the abode, the refuge and the most dear friend. I am the creation and the annihilation, the basis of everything, the resting place and the eternal seed.

O Arjuna, I give heat, I withhold and send forth the rain. I am immortality, and I am also death personified. Both spirit & matter are in me.

Those who study the Vedas and drink the soma juice, seeking the heavenly planets, worship Me indirectly. Purified of sinful reactions, they take birth on the pious, heavenly planet of Indra, where they enjoy godly delights.

When they have thus enjoyed vast heavenly sense pleasure and the results of their pious activities are exhausted, they return to this mortal planet again. Thus, those who seek sense enjoyment by adhering to the principles of the three Vedas achieve only repeated birth & death. But those who always worship Me with exclusive devotion, meditating on My transcendental form — to them I carry what they lack, and I preserve what they have.

Those who are devotees of other gods and who worship them with faith actually worship only Me. O son of Kunti, but they do so in a wrong way. I am the only enjoyer and master of all sacrifices. Therefore, those who do not recognize My true transcendental nature fall down. Those who worship the demigods will take birth among the demigods; those who worship the ancestors go to the ancestors; those who worship ghosts and spirits will take birth among such beings; and those who worship Me will live with Me.

THE OPULENCE OF THE ABSOLUTE

Krishna says he is the source of the Demigods and Sages and neither know My origin or opulence. I am also the source of all spiritual and material worlds; I am the unborn, the beginning less, and the supreme lord of all worlds. Every theory emanates from me. I am the supersoul, and consciousness (living force) seated in the hearts of the living, etc.

Only by devoting fully to Krishna can one understand & know Him & get enlightened.

Intelligence, knowledge, freedom from doubt and delusion, forgiveness, truthfulness, control of the senses, control of the mind, happiness & desires, birth, death, fear, fearlessness, nonviolence, equanimity, satisfaction, austerity, charity, fame & infamy - all these various qualities in living beings are created by Me alone.

I am the source of all spiritual and material worlds. I am the unborn, the beginningless, & Supreme Lord of all worlds. Everything emanates from me. The wise who know this engage in my devotional service and worship me with all their hearts.

I dwell in the hearts of my devotees shining them special mercy, destroying with the lamp of knowledge the darkness born of ignorance.

Arjuna said: You are the Supreme Personality of Godhead, the ultimate abode, the purest, the Absolute Truth. You are the eternal, transcendental original person, the unborn, the greatest; greater than all demigods.

Arjuna asks Krishna about his opulences: Krishna shows His main ones:

"I am the Supersoul, O Arjuna, seated in the hearts of all living creatures. I am the beginning, the middle and the end of all beings.

"Of the Adityas I am Vishnu, of light I am the radiant sun, of the Maruts, I am Marici and among the stars I am the moon.

Of the Vedas I am the Sama Veda; of the demigods I am Indra, the king of heaven; of the senses I am the mind; and in living beings I am the living force [consciousness].

Of all the Rudras I am Lord Siva, of the Yaksas and Raksasas I am the Lord of wealth [Kuvera], of the Vasus I am fire [Agni], and of mountains I am Meru.

Of priests, know Me to be the chief, Brhaspati. Of generals I am Kartikeya, and of bodies of water I am the ocean.

Of the great sages I am Bhrgu, of vibrations I am the transcendental Om. Of sacrifices I am the chanting of the holy names [japa], and of immovable things I am the Himalayas.

Of all trees I am the banyan tree, and of the sages among the demigods I am Narada. Of the Gandharvas I am Citraratha, and among perfected beings I am the sage Kapila.

Of horses know Me to be Uccaihsrava, produced during the churning of the ocean for nectar. Of lordly elephants I am Airavata, and among men I am the monarch.

Of weapons I am the thunderbolt, among cows I am the Surabhi. Of causes for procreation I am Kandarpa, the god of love, and of serpents I am Vasuki, etc. etc.

I am the all devouring death, and I am the generating principle of all that is yet to be. Among women I am fame, fortune, fine speech, memory, intelligence, steadfastness and patience. I am the generating seed of all existences. There is no being - moving or non-moving - that can exist without me.

But what need is there, Arjuna, for this detailed knowledge? With a single fragment of myself I pervade and support this entire universe.

THE UNIVERSAL FORM

Arjuna asks to see how Krishna has entered into this cosmic manifestation; and to see that form of the Lord.

Krishna gives Arjuna "divine" eyes so he can see Krishnas form (invisible to the normal eye). Arjuna saw unlimited mouths, unlimited eyes, unlimited wonderful visions; the form decorated with many celestial garlands, garments, ornaments and scents bore many divine upraised weapons. The radiance from hundreds of thousands of suns rising into the sky might resemble the effulgence of the supreme person. The unlimited expansions of the universe were situated in the Lord (though divided into many, many thousand). The demigods, Lord Shiva, Brahma and the sages are assembled in You. I am also the great destroyer [who favours the righteous - Pandavas].

> Krishna invites Arjuna to see his opulences, hundreds of thousands of varied divine and multicoloured forms.
>
> However, you cannot see Me with your present eyes. Therefore, I give you divine eyes. Behold My mystic opulence!
>
> Arjuna saw in that universal form unlimited mouths, unlimited eyes, unlimited wonderful visions. The form was decorated with many celestial ornaments and bore many divine upraised weapons. He wore celestial garlands and garments, and many divine scents were smeared over his body. All was wondrous, brilliant, unlimited, all-expanding.

If hundreds of thousands of suns were to rise at once into the sky, their radiance might resemble the effulgence of the Supreme Person in that universal form.

At that time Arjuna could see in the universal form of the Lord the unlimited expansions of the universe situated in one place although divided into many, many thousands.

Arjuna prays to the Lord.

Arjuna said: My dear Lord Krishna, I see assembled in Your body all the demigods and various other living entities. I see Brahma sitting on the lotus flower, as well as Lord Siva and all the sages and divine serpents.

You are the ultimate resting place of this Universe. You are inexhaustible, and You are the oldest. You are the maintainer of the eternal religion, the Personality of Godhead.

You are without origin, middle or end. Your glory is unlimited. You have numerous arms, and the sun and moon are Your eyes. I see you with blazing fire coming forth from your mouth, burning this entire universe by your own radiance.

Oh, mighty armed one, all the planets with their demigods are disturbed at seeing your great form, with its many faces, eyes, arms, thighs, legs, and bellies and Your many terrible teeth; and as they are disturbed, so am I.

I cannot keep my balance seeing thus Your blazing deathlike faces and awful teeth.

All sons of Dhrtarastra, along with their allied kings, and Bhisma, Drona, Kama — and our chief soldiers also — are rushing into Your fearful mouths. And some I see trapped with heads smashed between your teeth.

I see all people rushing full speed into your mouths, as mouths dash to destruction in a blazing fire.

Arjuna asks the Lord further.

The Supreme Personality of Godhead said: Time I am, I am also the great destroyer of the worlds, and I have come here to destroy all people. With the exception of you [the Pandavas], all the soldiers here on both sides will be slain.

Therefore, get up; prepare to fight and win glory.

Arjuna also asks to see Krishna in his Four-armed form, with helmeted head & with club, wheel, conch and lotus flower in his hands. Krishna says that he has shown Arjuna his forms & potency. Krishna says "My dear Arjuna, he who engages in My pure devotional service, free from contamination of fruitive activities and mental speculation, he who works for Me, who makes Me the supreme goal of his life, and who is friendly to every living being — he certainly comes to Me [& sees Me].

DEVOTIONAL SERVICE

Devotional service to Krishna is regarded as superior to devotional service to the impersonal Brahman, the unmanifested and demigods. Such devotees are very dear to Me (Krishna).

Krishna says: "Those whose fix their minds on My Personal form and are always engaged in worshiping Me with great and transcendental faith are considered by Me to be most perfect.

Others who worship the unmanifested, being equally disposed to everyone, such persons, engaged in the welfare of all, at last achieve Me, however it is more difficult & disturbing, if your mind is attached to the unmanifested, impersonal feature of the Supreme.

Meditating on Me, devotion to Me is best - for all who do I am the swift deliverer from the ocean of birth and death.

Fix your mind on me without deviation, then follow the regulative principles of bhakti- yoga. In this way develop a desire to attain me. If you are unable to do this try giving up all results of your work and try to be self-situated.

Meditation is better than knowledge and renunciation of the fruits of action is good for achieving peace of mind.

Those most dear to me are: 1) those not disturbed by anyone, who are equipoised in happiness and distress, fear and anxiety; 2) those not dependent on the ordinary course of activities, who are pure, expert, without cares, free from all pains, and not striving for some result.

Further, one who neither rejoices, who neither laments nor desires, one who renounces both auspicious and inauspicious things; one who is equal to friends & enemies, who is equipoised in honour & dishonour, heat & cold, happiness & distress, fame and infamy, who is always free from contaminating association, always silent & satisfied with anything, who does not care for any residence, who is fixed in knowledge and who is engaged in devotional service is dear to me.

Those who follow this imperishable path of devotional service and who completely engage themselves with faith, making Me the supreme goal are very, very dear to me.

NATURE, THE ENJOYER & CONSCIOUSNESS

---◆❋◆---

The body is the field which has 5 elements plus false ego, the unmanifested, the ten senses, and the mind and 5 sense objects - desire, hatred, happiness, distress, the aggregate, the life symptoms and convictions.

These are the field of activities and its interactions.

Qualities like humility, pridelessness, non-violence, tolerance, simplicity, approaching a bona-fide spiritual master, cleanliness, steadiness, self-control, renunciation of the objects of sense gratification, absence of false ego, detachment, freedom from entanglement with family, even-mindedness, devotion to Krishna, solitude and detachment from ordinary people, self-realization, search for the absolute truth, etc. are all "knowledge". The Supersoul is the original source of all senses and maintainer of all living things. The Lord is knowledge and the object and goal of knowledge.

Nature is said to be cause of all material causes and effects.

The soul neither does anything nor is entangled; it does not mix with the body, though situated in that body.

Arjuna said to Krishna, I wish to know about Prakrti (nature), Purusa (the enjoyer), and the field & the knower of the field, and of knowledge and the object of knowledge.

The body is called the field, and one who knows this body is called the knower of the field.

The five great elements, false ego, intelligence, the unmanifested, the senses, and the mind, the five sense objects - desire, hatred, happiness, distress, the aggregate, the life symptoms, & convictions - all these are considered, in summary, to be the field of activities & its interactions.

Humility; pridelessness; nonviolence; tolerance; simplicity; approaching a bona-fide spiritual master; cleanliness; steadiness; self-control; renunciation of the objects of sense gratification; absence of false ego; the perception of the evil of birth, death, old age & disease; detachment;

freedom from entanglement with children, wife, home & the rest; and even-mindedness amid pleasant and unpleasant events; constant & unalloyed devotion to me; aspiring to live in a solitary place; detachment from the general mass of people; accepting the importance of self-realization; & philosophical search for the Absolute Truth; all these I declare knowledge, and besides this is ignorance.

Krishna explains the knowable, knowing which you will taste the eternal. Brahman, the spirit, beginningless, & subordinate to Me, lies beyond the cause & effect of this material world.

The Supersoul exists everywhere - everywhere are His hands, legs, eyes, ears, heads & faces.

The Supersoul is the original source of all senses. He is unattached; maintainer of all living beings; He transcends the modes of nature, whilst at the same time being the master of all modes of material nature.

The Supersoul, though far away is near; though appearing to be divided among all beings He is never divided. Though He is the maintainer of every living entity, it is to be understood that He devours & develops all.

He is knowledge and the object and goal of knowledge. He is the source of light in all luminous objects. He is beyond the darkness in matter & is unmanifest. He is in everyone's heart.

Nature is said to be the cause of all material causes and effects; whereas the living entity is the cause of the various sufferings & enjoyments in the world.

3 modes of nature: The living entity's association with material nature is where he meets good & evil amongst various species.

Yet in the body there is another, a transcendental enjoyer who is Lord, the superior proprietor, who exist as the overseer and permitter, & who is known as the supersoul.

Learning / knowing the "material actions" of the 3 modes of nature is important.

Some perceive the Supersoul within themselves through meditation, others through the cultivation of knowledge, & still others through working without fruitive desire.

One who sees the Supersoul accompanying the individual soul in all bodies, & who understands that neither the soul nor the Supersoul within the destructible body is ever destroyed, actually sees.

One who sees the Supersoul equally present everywhere, in every living being, does not degrade himself by his mind. Thus, he approaches the transcendental destination.

One who can see all activities are performed by the body, which is created of material nature, and sees that the self does nothing, actually sees.

Those with the vision of eternity can see that the imperishable soul is transcendental, eternal, and beyond the modes of nature. Despite contact with the material body, O Arjuna, the soul neither does anything nor is entangled.

The sky, due to its subtle nature, does not mix with anything, although it is all- pervading. Similarly, the soul, situated in Brahman vision does not mix with the body, though situated in that body.

As the sun alone illuminates all this universe, so does the living entity, one within the body, illuminate the entire body by consciousness.

Those who see with eyes the difference between the body & the knower of the body, & can also understand the process of liberation from this bondage in material nature attain to the supreme goal.

THE 3 MODES OF MATERIAL NATURE

Goodness, passion and ignorance are the 3 modes of material nature. Goodness is purest and frees one from all sinful reactions. Goodness is purest & frees one from all sinful reactions - leading to sense of happiness & knowledge. The manifestations of the mode of goodness can be experienced when all the gates of the body are illuminated by knowledge - real knowledge develops - those situated here go upward to the higher planets.

Passion has unlimited desires and longings and the living being is bound to material fruitive actions. When there is an increase in the mode of passion the symptoms of great attachment, fruitive activity, intense endeavour, & uncontrollable desire & hankering develop. This leads to misery & those in the mode of passion live on the earthly planets.

Ignorance is the delusion of all embodied living beings, leading to madness, sleep and indolence. The mode of darkness, born of ignorance, is the delusion of all embodied living entities. The results of this mode are madness, indolence & sleep, which bind the conditioned soul.

When the gates of the body are illuminated by knowledge there is goodness and one goes to the higher plains. Passion predominance leads to fruitive actions, attachment, uncontrollable desires, etc and leads to misery.

Increased ignorance leads to ignorance, darkness, inertia, madness and illusion leading one to the hellish worlds.

The total material substance, called Brahman, is the source of birth, & it is Brahman that I impregnate, making possible the births of all living beings, O son of Bharata.

I am the seed-giving father (for all species of life).

The 3 modes of material nature are "goodness", "passion" & "ignorance".

There is competition for supremacy between the modes.

When one transcends the 3 modes of nature, he attains the Lord's spiritual nature.

He who seeks illumination (not shows it), he who is unwavering & undisturbed & remaining transcendental to the mode of "material quality" - he who regards alike happiness & distress, he who looks upon earth, stone & gold with an equal eye, he who is equal to the desirable & the undesirable, situated well in praise & blame, honour & dishonour; who treats alike both friend-enemy & who has renounced all material activities - such a person has transcended the modes of nature.

One who engages in full devotional service, unfailing in all circumstances, at once transcends the modes of material nature & thus comes to the level of Brahman.

And I am the basis of the impersonal Brahman, which is immortal, imperishable & eternal & is the constitutional position of ultimate happiness.

THE YOGA OF THE SUPREME PERSON

Materiality must be overcome by detachment.

One bound by the 6 senses cannot quit this body/ senses

There are 2 classes of beings - fallible (who exist) in the material world and infallible (who exist) in the spiritual world.

He who knows the supreme and engages in devotional service to Krishna is the "knower" of everything. This is stated in the Vedas too.

The person who knows the banyan tree is the knower of the Vedas.

The branches of this tree extend downward and upward, nourished by the 3 modes of material nature. The twigs are the objects of the senses. This tree also has roots going down, and these are bound to the fruitive actions of human society.

One must cut down this strongly rooted material tree with the weapon of detachment. Thereafter, one must seek that place from which, having gone, one never returns, and there surrender to that Supreme Personality of Godhead from whom everything began and from whom everything has extended since time immemorial.

One can quit this material body. Those who are free from false prestige, illusion and false association, who understand the eternal, who are done with material lust, who are freed from the dualities of happiness & distress, and who, un-bewildered, know how to surrender unto the Supreme Person attain to that eternal kingdom. That supreme abode of mine is not illumined by the sun or moon, nor by fire or electricity.

Those who reach it never return to this material world. In the living body one enjoys & is bound by the 6 senses / sense objects.

One can quit this body / senses, (the modes of nature binding him).

The splendour of the sun & moon comes from me. I enter into each planet, & by My energy they stay in orbit. I am the fire of digestion in the bodies of all living entities, and I join with the air of life, outgoing and incoming, to digest the 4 kinds of foodstuff.

I am seated in everyone's heart, from Me come remembrance, knowledge & forgetfulness. By all the Vedas I am to be known. Indeed, I am the compiler of Vedanta, and I am the knower of the Vedas.

There are 2 classes of beings - fallible (who exist) in the material world & "infallible" (who exist) in the spiritual world.

Besides these two, there is the greatest living personality, the Supreme Soul, the imperishable Lord Himself, who has entered the three worlds & is maintaining them.

Because I am transcendental, beyond both the fallible and the infallible, and because I am the greatest, I am celebrated both in the world and in the Vedas as that Supreme Power.

Whoever knows me as the Supreme Personality of Godhead, without doubting, is the knower of everything. He therefore engages himself in full devotional service to Me, O son of Bharata.

This is the most confidential part of the Vedic scriptures. Whoever understands this will become wise, and his endeavours will know perfection.

THE DIVINE & DEMONAIC NATURES

The 3 gates of hell are lust, anger and greed.

Godly men are endowed with divine nature and have good qualities like fearlessness, self-purification, spirituality, charitable, self-control, sacrificial, austerity, simplicity, non-violence, truthfulness, calmness (not anger), renunciation, tranquillity, gentleness, modesty, steady determination, vigour, forgiveness, fortitude, cleanliness, non-covetous, non-enviousness & has compassion for all living beings. Pride, arrogance, conceit, anger, harshness, ignorance, lust are qualities that belong to the demoniac nature/ persons; they can propagate and destroy.

> (The Supreme Personality of Godhead said) Fearlessness; purification of one's existence; cultivation of spiritual knowledge; charity; self-control; performance of sacrifice; study of the Vedas; austerity; simplicity; nonviolence; truthfulness; freedom from anger; renunciation; tranquillity; aversion to fault-finding; compassion for all living entities; freedom from covetousness; gentleness; modesty; steady determination; vigour; forgiveness; fortitude; cleanliness; and freedom from envy and from the passion for honour - these transcendental qualities, (O son of Bharata,) belong to godly men endowed with divine nature.
>
> Pride, arrogance, conceit, anger, harshness and ignorance - these qualities belong to those of demoniac nature (O son of Prtha).

Among the demoniac there is less sense of judgment; neither cleanliness nor proper behaviour, nor truth is found in them. They do not believe in God (who could be in control) & say the world is produced of sex desire and has no cause other than lust (to propagate & perpetuate existence).

The demoniac engage in unbeneficial, horrible works that can destroy the world. Taking shelter of insatiable lust and absorbed in the conceit of pride and false prestige, the demoniac, thus illusioned, are always sworn to unclean work, attracted by the impermanent.

They believe gratifying senses is the prime necessity of human Civilization. They live in anxiety & bound by the hundreds of thousands of desires & being absorbed in lust & anger secure money (by illegal means (sometimes)) for sense gratification.

They count their wealth, develop schemes to gather more. They destroy their "enemies", think they are Lord, enjoyer, perfect, powerful & happy. They perform sacrifices, give some to charity, & thus rejoice. Such persons are deluded by ignorance. Being too strongly attached to sense enjoyment they fall down to hell.

Bewildered by false ego, strength, pride, lust & anger, the demons become envious of the "Supreme" who is situated in their own bodies and in the bodies of others, and blaspheme against real religion. Such who are envious & mischievous, I cast into the ocean of material existence, into various demoniac species of life.

Attaining repeated birth amongst the species of demoniac life, such persons can never approach me & gradually sink down to the most abominable type of existence.

The 3 gates to this hell are: lust, anger & greed. They lead to the degradation of the soul & should be given up.

The divine / transcendental qualities are conducive to liberation, whereas the demoniac qualities make for bondage.

Those who act conducive to self-realization (via scriptures & religion) gradually attain the supreme destination.

THE DIVISIONS OF FAITH

Men in the mode of goodness worship the demigods; Those in the mode of passion worship the demons.

Those in the mode of ignorance worship ghosts and spirits.

Foods also fall into category of goodness, passion and ignorance.

Sacrifices as a matter of duty, desiring no reward are in the nature of goodness; sacrifices performed for some material benefit or for pride are in the mode of passion. Sacrifices without directive of scripture, without Vedic hymns or without distribution of prasadam or without faith are in the mode of ignorance.

Austerity performed with faith, not expecting material reward and for the sake of the Supreme is called austerity in goodness.

Penance performed out of pride, to gain respect or honour or part worship is in the mode of passion and not stable or permanent.

Penance out of foolishness, self-torture or to hurt others is in the mode of ignorance. Charity given out of duty is in the mode of goodness.

Charity performed with expectation of reward or fruitive result is in the mode of passion. Charity performed at an impure place or time to unworthy persons or without attention to respect is in mode of ignorance. One should chant "Om Tat Sat" (Om to attain supreme, tat - non-materiality, sat - devotional sacrifice)

Arjuna enquired of Krishna "what is the situation of those who do not follow the principles of scripture but worship according to their own imagination? Are they in goodness, in passion or in ignorance?

Krishna says that the living being is said to be of a particular faith (goodness, passion or ignorance) according to the modes of nature he acquires.

Men in the mode of goodness worship the Demigods; those in the mode of passion worship the demons; and those in the mode of ignorance worship ghosts and spirits.

Those who undergo severe austerities and penances not recommended in the scriptures, performing them out of pride & egotism, who are impelled by lust & attachment, who are foolish and who torture the material elements of the body as well as the Supersoul dwelling within, are to be known as Demons.

Even food one eats, sacrifices, austerities & charity fall within the 3 modes of nature.

Foods dear to those in the mode of goodness increase the duration of life, purify one's existence and give strength, health, happiness & satisfaction. Such foods are juicy, fatty, wholesome, and pleasing to the heart (perhaps not the fatty ones).

Bitter, sour, salty, hot, pungent, dry & burning food cause distress, misery & disease & are in the mode of passion.

Food prepared for more than 2 hours before being eaten, tasteless, decomposed or putrid food, and consisting of remnants & untouchable things are dear to those in mode of ignorance.

Sacrifice performed according to the direction of scriptures, as a matter of duty, by those who desire no reward, is of the nature of goodness.

Sacrifice performed for some material benefit, or for the sake of pride, is in the mode of passion.

Sacrifice performed without regard for the directions of scripture, without distribution of prasadam, without chanting of Vedic hymns and remuneration to the priests, and without faith is considered to be in the mode of ignorance.

Austerity of the body consists in worship of the Supreme Lord, the Brahmanas, the spiritual master, and superiors like the father & mother, and in cleanliness, simplicity, celibacy and nonviolence.

Austerity of speech consists in speaking words that are truthful, pleasing, beneficial, and not agitating to others, and also in regularly reciting Vedic literature.

Austerities of the mind are satisfaction, simplicity, gravity, self-control & purification of one's existence.

This threefold austerity performed with faith, without expecting material benefit but performed for the sake of the Supreme is called austerity in goodness.

Penance performed out of pride - for the sake of gaining respect, honour & worship is said to be in the mode of passion. It is neither stable nor permanent.

Penance performed out of foolishness, with self-torture or to destroy or injure others is said to be in the mode of ignorance.

Charity given out of duty, without expectation of return, at the proper time & place, and to a worthy person is considered to be in the mode of goodness.

Charity performed with the expectation of some return or with a desire for fruitive results, or grudgingly is said to be charity in the mode of passion.

Charity performed at an impure place, at an improper time, to unworthy persons, or without proper attention or respect is said to be in the mode of ignorance.

When performing sacrifice, charity & penance in accordance with scriptural regulations one should begin always with "Om" to attain the Supreme; "tat" - to get free from material entanglement, and "sat" for devotional sacrifice.

Say "Om tat sat".

Anything done as sacrifice, charity or penance without faith in the Supreme, O son of Pritha, is impermanent (it is called "asat", it is useless both in this life and the next).

ADDENDUM - THE PERFECTION OF RENUNCIATION

Renunciation is the giving up of (the fruits of) all material activities and giving up the results of all activities. Prescribed duties should never be renounced. Acts of sacrifice, charity and penance must be performed - they purify even the great souls. They should be performed as a matter of duty, without attachment or any expectation of result. It is impossible to give up all activities but he who renounces the fruit of action is truly renounced. Actions have 5 causes and factors

One who is not motivated by false ego, whose intelligence is not enlarged, is not bound by his actions (even if he kills like in the Mahabharata war). Knowledge by which ones undivided spiritual nature is seen in all living entities, though in innumerable forms is in the mode of goodness.

Knowledge by which one sees that in every different body there is a different type of living entity is in the mode of passion.

Knowledge where one is attached to one kind of work, meagre work, without knowledge of the truth is in the mode of darkness.

Action which is regulated or without seeking attachment, love or hatred, or desire for fruitive results is in the mode of goodness.

Action performed with great effort to satisfy ones desires and enacted from a sense of false ego is in the mode of passion.

Action performed in illusion, disregarding scriptural injunctions, and without concern for future bondage or for violence or distress caused to others is in the mode of ignorance. Understanding what is good or bad, what ought not to be done and what is to be feared and not feared, what is bonding and liberating is in the mode of goodness. Understanding which cannot distinguish between religion and irreligion is in the mode of passion. Understanding which considers irreligion to be religion or religion to be irreligion under the spell of illusion and darkness and strives in the wrong direction is in the mode of ignorance.

Arjuna asks Krishna about the purpose of renunciation and of the renounced order of life.

The renounced order is the giving up of all material activities and giving up the results of all activities is called renunciation.

There are 3 kinds of renunciation:

Acts of sacrifice, charity & penance are not to be given up; they must be performed; they purify even the great souls.

They should be performed as a matter of duty, without attachment or any expectation of result.

Prescribed duties should never be renounced.

If one gives up his prescribed duties because of illusion, such renunciation is said to be in the mode of ignorance.

Anyone giving up prescribed duties as troublesome or out of fear of bodily discomfort is said to have renounced in the mode of passion.

When one performs prescribed duties only because they ought to be done, and renounces all material association and all attachment to fruit, his renunciation is said to be in the mode of goodness.

It is impossible for an embodied being to give up all activities, but he who renounces the fruits of action is truly renounced.

For one who is not renounced, the threefold fruits of action - desirable, undesirable - mixed - accrue after death. But those who are in the renounced order of life have no such result to suffer or enjoy.

There are 5 causes and factors for all actions, whether by body, mind or speech.

Therefore, one who thinks himself the only doer, not considering the five factors, is certainly not very intelligent & cannot see things as they are.

One who is not motivated by false ego, whose intelligence is not entangled, though he kills men in this world, does not kill; nor is he bound by his actions [as espoused in the Mahabharata war between the Pandavas and the Kauravas].

Knowledge, the object of knowledge, and the knower are the three factors that motivate action; the senses, the work and the doer are the constituents of action.

According to the 3 different modes of material nature, there are 3 kinds of knowledge, action & performance of action:

Knowledge by which one undivided spiritual nature is seen in all living entities, though divided in innumerable forms, is understood to be in the mode of goodness.

That knowledge by which one sees that in every different body there is a different type of living entity one should understand to be in the mode of passion.

That knowledge by which one is attached to one kind of work as the all in all, without knowledge of the truth, and which is very meagre, is said to be in the mode of darkness.

Action performed which is regulated & without attachment, without love or hatred, without desire for fruitive results is said to be in the mode of goodness.

Action performed with great effort to satisfy one's desires, & enacted from a sense of false ego, is called action in the mode of passion.

Action performed in illusion, in disregard of scriptural injunctions, & without concern for future bondage or for violence or distress caused to others is said to be in the mode of ignorance.

One who performs his duty without association with the modes of material nature, without false ego, with great determination & enthusiasm, & without wavering in success or failure is said to be a worker in the mode of goodness.

The worker who is attached to work & the fruits of work, desiring to enjoy those fruits, & who is greedy, always envious, impure, and moved by joy & sorrow, is said to be in the mode of passion.

The worker who is engaged in work against the injunctions of the scripture, who is materialistic, obstinate, cheating & expert in insulting others, & who is lazy, always morose & procrastinating is said to be a worker in the mode of ignorance.

The different kinds of understanding & determination, according to the 3 modes of material nature are:

That understanding by which one knows what ought to be done & what ought not to be done, what is feared & what is not feared, what is binding & what is liberating, is in the mode of goodness.

That understanding which cannot distinguish between religion & irreligion, between action that should be done and action that should not be done, is in the mode of passion.

That understanding which considers irreligion to be religion & religion to be irreligion, under the spell of illusion & darkness, & strives in the wrong direction, is in the mode of ignorance, O son of Pritha.

Determination that is unbreakable, sustained with steadfastness by yoga practice, thus controls the activities of the mind, life & senses is in the mode of goodness.

Determination by which one holds fast to fruitive results in religion, economic development & sense gratification is of the nature of passion.

Determination which cannot go beyond dreaming, fearfulness, lamentation, moroseness - illusion - is in the mode of darkness.

The 3 kinds of happiness are:

Awakening one to self-realization is in the mode of goodness.

Happiness derived from contact with senses & their objects, which appears like nectar at first but poison later is in the mode of passion.

Happiness which is blind to self-realization, which is delusion from beginning to end & which arises from sleep, laziness & illusion is said to be of the mode of ignorance.

These 3 modes born of material nature apply to all beings, whether here or among the demigods in the higher planetary systems.

The qualities of Brahmanas, Kshatriyas, Vaisyas & Sudras traditionally are:

Brahmanas: peacefulness, self-control, austerity, purity, tolerance, honesty, knowledge, wisdom & religiousness

Kshatriyas: heroism, power, determination, resourcefulness, courage in battle, generosity & leadership

Vaisyas: farming, cow protection & business

Sudras: labour and service to others

One can attain perfection through work:

It is better to engage in one's own occupation even though one may be performing it imperfectly, than to accept another's occupation & do it well; better to engage in duties prescribed to one's nature & free from sinful reactions.

One who is self-controlled & unattached & disregards all material enjoyments can obtain by practice of renunciation, the highest perfect stage of freedom from reaction.

Achieving this perfection can lead to Brahman.

Being purified by his intelligence & controlling the mind with determination, giving up the objects of sense gratification, being freed from attachment & hatred, living in a secluded place, eating little, controlling the body, mind & power of speech, being in a trance & being detached, free from false ego, false strength, false pride, lust, anger & acceptance of material things, free from false proprietorship, being peaceful - such a person is elevated to the position of self-realization.

He realizes the Supreme Brahman & becomes fully joyful; He never laments or desires to have anything; He is equally disposed toward every living entity. In such state he attains pure devotional service to Me.

One can understand God by devotional service.

Though engaged in all kinds of activities, My pure devotee, under My protection, reaches the eternal & imperishable abode by My grace.

In all activities just depend on Me (God), work under My protection & work with devotion & conscious of Me.

If you become conscious of Me, you will pass over all the obstacles of conditioned life by My grace, otherwise acting with false ego & not hearing Me you will be lost.

If you do not act according to My direction & do not fight, then you will be falsely directed. By your nature, you will have to be engaged in warfare. The Supreme Lord is situated in everyone's heart, O Arjuna, & is directing the wanderings of all living entities, who are seated as on a machine, made of the material energy. Surrender to Him (Lord) & by His grace you will attain transcendental peace & the supreme & eternal abode.

I have bestowed on you this confidential knowledge, deliberate on it & then do what you wish to do.

Hear from Me My supreme instructions.

Always think of Me, become My devotee, worship Me, & offer your homage to Me. Thus, you will come to Me.

Abandon all varieties of religion & just surrender to Me; I shall deliver you from all sinful reactions; do not fear.

This confidential knowledge is only for the austere, devoted, & non-envious of Me.

For one who explains this supreme secret to the devotees, pure devotional service is guaranteed, & at the end he will come back to Me. Such a person is most dear to Me.

One who listens with faith & without envy becomes free from sinful reactions & attains to the auspicious planets where the pious dwell.

O son of Prtha, O conqueror of wealth, have you heard this with an attentive mind? Are your ignorance & illusions now dispelled?

Arjuna says his illusion is now gone & he has gained his memory of the Lord's mercy, that he is now firm & free from doubt & prepared to act according to the Lord's instructions.

Such wonderful dialogue between 2 great souls Krsna & Arjuna.

Where there is Krsna, the master of all mystics, & wherever there is Arjuna, the supreme archer, there will also certainly be opulence, victory, extraordinary power & morality.

www.ingramcontent.com/pod-product-compliance
Lightning Source LLC
Chambersburg PA
CBHW071936020426
42331CB00010B/2904